An Introduction to
Coping with
Depression
for Carers

Tony Frais

ROBINSON
London

ROBINSON

Published in Great Britain in 2015 by Robinson

Copyright © Tony Frais, 2015

The moral right of the author has been asserted.

Important Note
This book is not intended as a substitute for medical advice
or treatment. Any person with a condition requiring medical
attention should consult a qualified medical practitioner
or suitable therapist.

A CIP catalogue record for this book
is available from the British Library.

ISBN: 978-1-47211-933-9 (paperback)
ISBN: 978-1-47211-934-6 (ebook)

Typeset in Palatino by Initial Typesetting Services, Edinburgh
Printed and bound in Great Britain by
CPI Group (UK) Ltd, Croydon, CR0 4YY

Papers used by Robinson are from well-managed forests
and other responsible sources

MIX
Paper from
responsible sources
FSC® C104740
www.fsc.org

Robinson
is an imprint of
Constable & Robinson Ltd
100 Victoria Embankment
London EC4Y 0DY

An Hachette UK Company
www.hachette.co.uk

www.littlebrown.co.uk

For my wife, Helen.

For all her love, support and
encouragement.

Foreword

This excellent guide leads the reader through the different stages of the carer's and patient's journey through the experience of depression. The guide balances empathy with the challenges they are facing alongside clarity about what to expect and practical strategies for managing situations as they arise. There are key messages about the importance of the carer looking after their own health and well-being in order to be able to support the patient and work in partnership with them to overcome depression. It is an honest insight underpinned by the author's own experiences and whilst the emphasis is on the carer, it is a guide that is equally valuable to the patient themselves and their wider family and friends in facilitating an understanding of the experience of depression.

Elaine McNichol

Academic Lead for Service User
and Carer Involvement

University of Leeds

Contents

CONTENTS

Introduction

This booklet has been designed to help those caring for someone with depression. You may not describe yourself as a carer, you may be the depressed person's spouse, sibling, parent, child or friend. The term carer is used in the broadest sense as someone who is offering support and care to someone experiencing depression.

Depression is a seriously disabling illness affecting 10% of the population. But it is not only the depressed person with a problem. The effects of the illness also impact on the person's carers. Carers are suddenly thrust in to caring for a person suffering from an illness they barely understand. The carer begins to lead a life which can at times be overwhelming and demanding. Normal social and family life can be disrupted. As the illness progresses, many carers report feelings of being worn down physically and mentally from the stress of caring as well as not being able to plan for the future. They also experience a sense of hopelessness, frustration and annoyance, and feel neglected and isolated. As a result of this, there is the danger that carers could also become depressed.

But caring for a depressed person may not necessarily be a negative experience in every case. Carers can and do find a positive meaning to their role and are able to achieve a purposeful, rewarding and effective quality of care which can not only benefit the depressed person but can also lead to reduced levels of stress for the carer.

So the issue is just how carers can best deal with the situation they suddenly find themselves in; what the future holds and how they can best help the depressed person and themselves.

As someone caring for a person with depression, you will be faced with seeing them through their illness. However, it is also important to think about your own well-being.

Each part of this booklet describes the significant stages of the carer's and depressed person's journey through the experience of depression.

The booklet includes the thoughts of real life carers and depressed people who best capture their emotions at points of time during the course of the illness.

Throughout this booklet, the carer and the depressed person are considered as partners who are facing this experience together.

Part 1 The nature of depression

As a first step towards successful caring, it is

important that the carer has a good under-standing of the nature of depression and how it affects the person.

Part 2 The impact of depression on carers

This section discusses how the first experi-ences of looking after a depressed person may begin to have an impact on your life.

Part 3 Seeking help and support

How carers can begin to seek the help and support they need.

Part 4 Stigma and seeking treatment

This discusses how the stigma of depres-sion can often be a barrier to people seeking treatment.

Part 5 Visiting the GP

This section details what you might experi-ence when the depressed person agrees to visit their GP. Although many patients are happy to have someone with them at their GP consultation, some patients may be unwilling to involve the carer. The GP has a duty of confidentiality to the patient. The issues regarding the medication prescribed by the GP are also discussed.

Part 6 What happens if the treatment given by the GP is not helping?

Research has shown that approximately 35% of depressed patients respond to antidepressant medication prescribed by their GP. For those who prefer psychological approaches, most areas of the UK have access to psychological treatment services often known as Improving Access to Psychological Treatment (IAPT) services. Your GP will be able to refer you. If these approaches don't help, then the depressed person can be referred to what is known as secondary care and will be seen by the mental health team. However, success in finding new and effective treatment that might be helpful for the patient is not guaranteed. This may be the most difficult time for both carer and patient.

Part 7 Recovery and relapse prevention

Recovery from depression marks a time that is just as crucial as any other time during the course of the illness for both carer and patient. A large percentage of patients remain vulnerable to relapses. In order to lessen the chance of relapse, it is important that the patient receives ongoing treatment such as talking therapy in addition to remaining on their medication.

Part 8 Care for the carer

How you can access advice and support in order to protect your own health and well-being.

Part 9 The positives of caring

Despite the stresses and difficulties, caring can turn out to be a positive experience.

Key points to remember

Useful websites for advice and support

References

Part 1:

THE NATURE OF DEPRESSION

As a carer, you will be better prepared to face the challenges ahead if you have a good understanding of the nature of the illness. Understanding depression will help you cope with the changes in the person's behaviour and reactions.

The experience of and attitudes towards suffering from depression inevitably vary between different people. However, there are a number of common threads in terms of symptoms. The Royal College of Psychiatrist's leaflet 'Working in Partnership with Psychiatrists and Carers', lists the following symptoms, which, if continuing for more than a few weeks, indicate a depressive episode.

Changes in the person's behaviour

As a carer, you may notice that the person:

- is unhappy most of the time
- has lost confidence in themselves
- expresses feelings of guilt, shame and worthlessness
- is irritable and, perhaps, angry
- is tearful
- has lost their appetite, or eats more than usual
- has changed their sleeping pattern
- is extremely tired
- has problems concentrating
- looks and feels anxious

is withdrawn and has lost interest in life, including sex

 isn't looking after themselves as well as usual

 is feeling suicidal.

Episodes of depression can last an average of four to eight months but there can be cases where it lasts for longer. Sometimes depression can be a direct result of personal difficulties such as the loss of a loved one, mounting financial problems or unemployment. It can also be the result of suffering a physical illness such as a heart attack, diabetes or cancer.

Depression may at times have roots that stem from these catastrophic life events but it can also be a result of increasing negativity about life in general. When people become depressed, they may also begin to stop feeling any enjoyment in doing what they previously liked to do, and they may exhibit a growing uncertainty about their future prospects in life. Such feelings may be dismissed by the person as no more than just being a bit fed up and nothing more serious than that.

However, this insidious build-up of increasingly negative thinking begins to undermine and adversely affect the person's behaviour and mood, which can lead to the descent into depression. When this happens, and it can sometimes happen very suddenly, it leaves the person frightened and bewildered; they cannot understand what is happening to them or why.

Depression is an experience that is almost impossible to compare with any physical illness. Depressed people often become frustrated at not being able adequately to convey to family and friends just what a terrible experience it is. The depressed person becomes suspended in time; they do not consider the future and have difficulty in remembering the past. Instead they focus entirely on their present emotional state.

Depressed people may have difficulty managing everyday affairs; they may lack a sense of meaning, have few goals or aims, and lack a sense of direction. They are likely to become uninterested in life, and unable to develop new attitudes or behaviours.[1]

Depressed people's memories can also be affected. They may struggle to recall happier times from the past. They may tend to dwell only on remembered times of sadness or failure. Many will also brood too much on their own distress. It can be difficult for depressed people to escape from this cycle of negative thinking.

Despite initial urging from friends and family, it is impossible for the depressed person to just 'snap out of it'. For many people, this locked-in pattern of misery cannot even be changed by pleasures such as going on a luxury holiday or winning some money on the Lottery.

Nothing highlights the depths of suffering more than the fact that depressed people at some point often think of suicide as a way out of their misery because they cannot believe that things will get better, cannot stand the pain of depression, and, in some cases, even believe that other people will genuinely be better off without them.

Anxiety

A large percentage of depressed people have high levels of anxiety. This is a significant and important feature that needs to be understood in order to develop a more complete picture of the nature of depression. It is widely accepted that anxiety and depression go hand in hand. Anxiety affects people in different ways. Depressed people may spend a long time worrying about what might happen and find it difficult to switch this worrying off. Anxiety also affects the body. Physical sensations such as a racing heart, difficulties in breathing and a feeling of butterflies in the stomach contribute to making depression a physically uncomfortable illness in addition to its adverse psychological effects.

Diurnal variations – the false recovery

There is an unusual and not-well-understood aspect to the nature of depression. This is the phenomenon of diurnal variations. Diurnal means something that happens on a daily basis. A daily variation in mood has been recognized as a characteristic feature in the more severe cases of depression. The depressed person who experiences diurnal variations typically faces low mood in the morning but improved mood towards the evening, though there are cases where mood is better in the morning and becomes worse in the evening. During these periods, the person may believe they have finally overcome their illness. However, this 'recovery' is often a false dawn and the full weight of the symptoms invariably returns the next day. There may be cases where a 'recovery' of this type can last for a few days but, again, symptoms return, much to the disappointment of the depressed person.

Part 2:

THE IMPACT OF DEPRESSION ON CARERS

Most carers are completely unprepared for living and coping with a person suffering from depression. The fact that depression is a mysterious and complex illness that cannot be easily explained or described makes it difficult for both the carer and the depressed person to convey to others what they are experiencing. It is also an illness that some people may think trivial, and you may find that family and friends do not fully appreciate the impact it is having on your life.

Depressed people may sometimes talk openly about feeling suicidal. Any such talk of suicide should not be taken lightly, but during the early stages of the illness it is possible that it may simply be a way in which the person is trying to convey to the carer the depth of their suffering. Circumstances where there may be a more serious risk of suicide, and what to do about this, are discussed in Chapter 6.

As the illness progresses, other distressing aspects for carers include: being upset by the depressed person's irritability and lack of interest, and feeling discouraged by an increasing sense of hopelessness and concern about their future. Social life also begins to be affected.

> 'She didn't want to go out, so we didn't go out. We'd knock back invitations . . . then they stopped coming, so we stayed home.'[2]

Expressing concern to the depressed person that they are not behaving like their normal

26

selves, and asking whether something is wrong, is often a useful first step. It is helpful if you can encourage the depressed person to talk about their feelings and emotions as early as possible.

This would signify to them that there is a genuine desire to try and understand what is going on; what they are thinking about and why. The intention is to make it clear that you are an active partner and willing to give all the help and support possible in overcoming the illness.

One study describes the experience of caring for a depressed person and the impact it had on the life of the carer. Many carers reported feelings of anxiety and exhaustion.

'There is constant emotional tension . . . every day I wake up and think – what is going to happen today, what will they be like?'

'You come home from work, you get changed and you're on. It's like working double shifts.' 'You have to be ever-vigilant . . . every day there is a potential crisis.'

'You live each day feeling like you're walking on eggshells. I didn't know what to say to him, to make him feel better. But I was also afraid of saying anything at all because any little thing could have made him feel worse.'

'You can only keep propping the other person up for so long, then you feel deflated and exhausted . . . and then you start to feel down.'[3]

Another issue you may experience is a lack of positive feedback from the depressed person as to whether your contribution and efforts are being appreciated. There may also be times when you feel upset because the depressed person takes their anger and frustration out on you. However, it is important to remember that this hostility is more a result of the illness and not their normal personality.

Although you may make every effort to comfort the depressed person, the nature of depression is such that there will be times when they may simply want to be left alone for a period of time, as one carer found:

'The way I look at it, if you care for a person, you've got to let them be who they want to be at that time. If they want to talk, they talk. If they don't want to talk, they don't talk. If they just want to sit there and stare into space, but as long as you are there for them.'[3]

Communication

As the illness progresses, normal conversation between you and the person may begin to break down. As one depressed person explained:

'It is not the relationship that existed prior to the illness . . . So the things that you talk about in a relationship which are around plans for the future . . . about the children and where you might go on holiday or . . . what's happening in the world or what's happened today. You don't have any of those conversations, because the person with the depression has no interest in those conversations . . . So actually it's a very lonely period.'[3]

Achieving effective communication as soon as possible between yourself and the depressed person is important. The ability to be open with one another, share feelings and thoughts, can be one of the keys to success. But achieving meaningful communication may not be easy. If you do not have early success, there is the danger that you may become frustrated and feel less inclined to try and communicate with them. However, these difficulties can be overcome.

In the first instance, you need to be aware that depressed people often have a short attention span, which means effective communication may only be possible in frequent but brief conversations. However, there will also be times when symptoms are so severe that the depressed person will find it almost impossible to talk. The timing of communication between you both is therefore crucial.

When symptoms become less severe and the depressed person seems to be more approachable, this could be the time to have a more relaxed conversation. Depressed people may find that being able to talk to you about their feelings in a meaningful way can be emotionally beneficial. As one person describes it:

'Talking gets my frustrations and anger out . . . It takes a load off . . . it calms me down . . . You're not quite so on your own. You don't feel quite so isolated. I think you just come out of your hole a bit.'[3]

31

Being able to talk to the depressed person without being judgemental or critical will be appreciated. But what effective communication can also do is establish that both of you are on the same side; a united effort with the aim of overcoming the illness.

Family and friends

Inevitably, family and close friends become aware that there are problems and, with the best intentions, they may want to try and help as best they can. However, there are challenges to overcome.

You are likely to be faced with trying to describe what the depressed person is going through. They are also likely to be mystified by the situation.

As some carers explain:

'They just don't know how to handle it
. . . it's not their fault, you can't blame
them . . .'[3]

'People are ignorant about mental
illness; they don't understand it.
They can sympathize or empathize
with a caregiver for someone with cancer or dementia or a stroke, but they
just don't get mental illness. They
don't appreciate how difficult it is to be
in this position.'[4]

Can the support of family and friends make a difference? They can certainly be a great help if they have a good understanding of what the depressed person is going through, in order to provide the right emotional and sympathetic support; it is important to demonstrate that they care, listen in a non-judgemental way and are prepared to keep what they see and hear confidential. The depressed person may appreciate this support because family and friends can sometimes give a fresh perspective on the situation other than that of the carer. Encouraging family support can also be helpful to your mental and physical health. Having understanding and helpful family and friends can be invaluable, particularly as some carers may be reluctant to ask for support. While there may not be any sign of appreciation of your efforts from the depressed person, support from family and friends can help the carer to feel valued. As one carer remarks:

> 'I get compliments from friends and relatives – I never get any from the patient.'[5]

However, if family and friends are not aware of how depression can affect someone, they may say things that are likely to upset and annoy the depressed person such as 'You have a wonderful quality of life so how can you be feeling this way?' They may also suggest they should be putting more effort into getting themselves better. In addition, the depressed person may be concerned that some of the family and friends may gossip to others about their condition.

Young carers

Living with and caring for a depressed person inevitably has its stressful effects on younger family members. It can put a huge strain on the relationship that the child has with the family member who is depressed and can have a long-term negative impact.

Some young carers may feel that they have lost their close relationship with the depressed parent. They may also notice how the illness affects the way their parents behave towards one another, or the different demands each of them makes. There may also be times when a young carer's life can become one of constant worry and isolation. Children will often find it difficult to explain to their friends and fellow school pupils what is happening in their lives and how it is affecting them, which may result in a degree of withdrawal as they feel less inclined to take part in normal social activities. In addition, the stigma attached to depression can result in children keeping what they are experiencing to themselves.

To lessen the impact the illness has on them, your children may cope better and perhaps have a more positive attitude towards the situation if you explain the nature of the illness in an age-appropriate way; talk about how it affects the depressed person and encourage them to discuss with you their worries and fears at all times. It is important to encourage conversations as early as possible once your children begin to notice that the depressed person is behaving in a way they do not understand or recognize. Young carers need to be reassured that it is not their fault and they have no reason to feel guilty. It may also be helpful if they are made to feel part of the family caring team. Getting in touch with a healthcare professional, such as a school nurse, and asking them to have a conversation with your children may well be useful. Above all, it is important for the family to try and regularly do 'normal things as a family'.

There are many local and national organizations devoted to the welfare of young carers that will connect them to young carer services and online support. They can also be connected to young carer groups, which can give them someone to talk to and enable them to meet other young people in similar circumstances. It is often important for the young carer to have someone outside the family to talk to such as a young carer support worker.

It is vital that your child gets this support as soon as possible before they become too badly affected by what is happening in their lives.

Trust and acceptance

Achieving a level of trust between you and the depressed person from the beginning of the illness may prove to be helpful.

Trust means that you and the depressed person have confidence in each other; that you will try and do your best for them and that they will be respected and listened to without being judged or criticized. Having trust in one another is the fundamental basis needed for successful teamwork in which you and the depressed person share common goals – the welfare and well-being of both. As one depressed person commented:

> 'If you trust someone . . . you're half-way there.' [3]

Accepting that there is a limit to how much you can improve the person's condition for the better can also be helpful for the carer. In his book *Speaking of Sadness*, which details the effects of depression, David Karp tells of his appreciation for his wife's concern but also of being upset at her incomprehension of his condition. He describes his wife's eventual realization that:

> 'Nothing she could say or do would make much of a difference; even worse, efforts to comfort me might only invite more negativity.'[6]

Carers find they have more peace of mind when they accept that:

> 'I did not cause it. I cannot control it. I cannot cure it. All I can do is cope with it.'[7]

Part 3:

SEEKING HELP
AND SUPPORT

There are things you need to do to gain help and support for yourself.

Early help and support is vital because the person's depression may last for some time and this could take a heavy toll on your own well-being. A useful first step is to talk to your GP to let them know that you are caring for someone with depression. This can be recorded on your medical records, and will help the GP to provide support to you when needed.

There is little point stumbling along and learning on the job, so you need to talk to other people who are in similar circumstances. In order to do this, you should consider contacting the local carers' advice centre as soon as possible in order to prepare and plan for the difficult times that may lie ahead. You can get in touch with your local centre by visiting the websites of national carer organizations such as Carers UK and Carers Trust, which will give you advice and information as to where your nearest carer advice centre is and how you can arrange a visit to discuss the problems you are having. The websites of these and other carer organizations are listed at the end of this booklet. If you do not have access to a computer, your local library will be able to help.

These centres are a good source for help, advice, understanding and support. Carers will appreciate being able to speak to someone who listens.

Arrangements can also be made to meet and talk with other carers about how they are coping and which strategies they find work best. As some carers discovered:

'You need to be able to talk [about] what's going on with other people . . . you need that respite in order to provide the right sort of support. Because I think every time you do that, you come back with a refreshed . . . energy level and tolerance level.'[3]

'It's been so beneficial to me being involved in carers groups . . . just hearing everybody's story, and realising . . . hang on – I'm not the only one going through this.'[3]

Quite often, the person experiencing the depression will be the one who generally deals with the bills and other financial matters. You might find yourself in the situation where the person with depression can no longer cope with this responsibility. Carers' centres can provide practical advice to help you before the situation begins to get out of hand.

While learning from other carers' experiences and other sources can be helpful to some degree, the fact is that each depressed person experiences and reacts to the illness in their own individual way; a way that is unique to them. The same goes for the carer; the strategies employed and their reactions to situations can differ with each individual carer. Therefore, it is likely that what works best for one carer may not necessarily work for another, meaning that in certain cases it may come down to you having to decide what works best by trial and error. As one carer discovered:

> 'It was a sort of trial and error, that's the way it felt to me . . . So . . . I don't know whether it's the right thing or not, well let's try it. Oh, it doesn't seem to work, well let's try something else.'[3]

There can even be cases where what is working best for you and the depressed person one day may not work the next day. As one carer experienced:

44

> '1 could use the same techniques to try and deal with the situation that had . . . worked perfectly the night before . . . and get a completely different response.'[3]

Discovering new strategies which may work is one thing but seeking professional medical advice is another important step in getting the right treatment for the depressed person. However, there may be times when, for their own reasons, some people are reluctant to seek treatment.

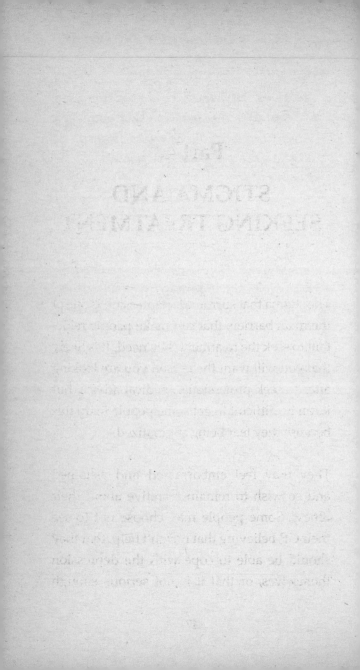

Part 4:

STIGMA AND SEEKING TREATMENT

The stigma that surrounds depression is one of the main barriers that can make people reluctant to seek the treatment they need. It is likely that you will want the person you are looking after to seek professional medical advice, but it can be difficult to get some people to do this because they fear being stigmatized.

They may feel embarrassed and ashamed and so wish to remain secretive about their illness. Some people may choose not to see their GP, believing that it won't help, that they should be able to cope with the depression themselves, or that it is not serious enough to justify seeking treatment. There may also be worries that their illness will go onto their medical record, and may prejudice their present or future employment. However, a number of organizations are now running active anti-stigma campaigns aimed at changing negative attitudes among the general public and employers. Recently, a number of well-known celebrities have been open about suffering from depression, which has gone a long way in de-stigmatizing the illness.

Another issue for the depressed person can be the taking of medication, particularly anti-depressants. Some may have concerns about possible side effects associated with these and others believe that continued use will lead to addiction.

Persuading the person with depression to seek treatment

The importance of getting the earliest possible treatment is accurately summed up by the words of a depressed person who in hindsight admitted that:

> 'Everyone says "but you look so well", you know, "you look great", and "there's nothing wrong, don't be silly" . . . maybe if I got help earlier, if someone had identified it and treated it more seriously, things would have been better.'[8]

The problem lies in trying to persuade the person to agree that seeking treatment as soon as possible is a positive and necessary step towards recovery.

There are ways to gently persuade the reluctant person to seek treatment:

> 'If they don't seem to be bothering to get any kind of treatment, maybe a gentle reminder would do. They say that,

sometimes, people are more open to sug-
gestions after they've thought about
things for a while. And maybe if a bit
more time goes by with nothing happening, another gentle reminder might
work.[9]

Perhaps make the point that if a depressed person is seriously interested in getting better, seeking medical advice and treatment could be an important step towards recovery.

When symptoms are less intense could be one of the better opportunities to have a serious discussion about what you feel the person should do.

Part 5:

VISITING THE GP

With symptoms of depression still persisting, the person has decided or been successfully persuaded by you that the time has come to visit the GP. If you can, it will always be helpful to accompany them.

On seeing the GP, the important thing is effective communication between the GP and patient. There may be cases where depressed patients have difficulty opening up to their GP to express their problems and emotions in a meaningful way. It may be difficult for the patient to explain what they are going through because depression is something of a mystery to them. They find it hard to explain in words how they are feeling. However, you can have an important role to play in assisting them to give the GP a full picture of what is happening, especially as it is you who knows the patient best. In addition, depression can affect the patient's memory, so you might have to fill in the gaps in the story, supplying details that the patient has forgotten to mention to the GP. In this way, you can improve the quality of care the patient receives from the GP. It is likely that when you are considered a 'partner in care' by the GP, you will feel a greater sense of purpose and importance, which should also help you feel more confident about your abilities and more in control of the situation.

Patients are frequently concerned about taking up the GP's time. They may feel guilty that there are other patients waiting to see the GP, and thus rush through their appointment. One patient sums this up well: 'It is as if you are making a fuss really ... and you don't have very long to actually speak to them, they have only got a certain time. So you haven't got enough time to actually, you know, make them understand and for it to come across exactly how you feel.'[10]

Some GPs may recognize that the average consultation time is insufficient for an in-depth discussion with the patient and offer a longer appointment. Being listened to by the GP is a major issue for patients. Most place great value on a GP who is prepared to listen and show recognition and understanding of their condition. Patients believe that if they are listened to, they are being valued as a person, and they gain a sense that their problems are understood.

Once the GP has diagnosed that the patient is suffering from depression, the next step is to decide what form of treatment will be offered. In the majority of cases, GPs may decide on treatment with antidepressants, as medical guidelines recommend this as the first-line treatment for depression. Antidepressants can be helpful in some cases, but there is an important issue that needs to be thought about. Sometimes taking a pill can make people feel that they have an illness that is going to be medically treated, and thus that any personal involvement in their recovery may not be necessary. It's important to emphasize that some depressed patients can still do a great deal to help themselves, and to tackle their problems.

Some patients may have strong reservations about taking antidepressants and may prefer to try talking treatments first. If the GP decides that talking therapy is appropriate, they can refer the patient to a talking therapist. The most common form of talking therapy is cognitive behavioural therapy (CBT). CBT sets out to help the person to understand how depressed mood, thinking and behaviour all interact together in negative cycles, and to help change the ways patients think and behave so that their mood can improve. Counselling is a type of talking therapy; it involves the patient talking about their problems to a counsellor who will listen sympathetically and help the depressed person to work through their feelings, often about difficult issues in their lives or problems that resulted in the depression in the first place.

There can sometimes be delays before the patient gets to see a therapist or counsellor, but access to talking therapy is slowly improving under the NHS programme Improving Access to Psychological Therapies.

Confidentiality

Not all people want their carer to accompany them on their visit to the GP, which can make it hard for the carer to know what treatment the GP has recommended. The GP has a duty of confidentiality, which means that what has been said and the treatments and advice given to the patient will not be revealed to the carer unless the patient agrees that the GP can share this information. There can be cases where the GP may be uneasy about sharing information with a carer and some may refuse to do so at all. But the GP should recognize that being excluded from the treatment process may make many carers feel undervalued and irrelevant. Carers who are sympathetic to the needs of the patient should be made to feel that they are part of the solution rather than the problem. Official guidelines for healthcare professionals state:

Issues around confidentiality should not be used as a reason for not listening to carers, nor for not discussing fully with service users the need for carers to receive information so that they can continue to support them. Carers should be given sufficient information, in a way they can readily understand, to help them provide care efficiently.[11]

As a carer, you are entitled to see the GP on your own and raise any concerns you have about the patient and, just as importantly, your own well-being.

Carers indicate that ideally they and the person with the illness should be consulted independently as well as together. This is seen to greatly assist the carer with respect to management issues, yet allow the person with the illness to have privacy.[12]

If the GP cannot inform the carer because of confidentiality, this may affect the quality of care the patient receives from the carer. If the GP believes the carer ought to be part of the treatment process, it is up to them to persuade the patient that it would be in their best interests to have the carer become more involved in the patient's welfare and treatment.

Medication and compliance

Because antidepressant treatment for depression is the rule rather than the exception, the issues surrounding whether the patient is taking medication as prescribed are important for both patient and carer. There are a number of different types and brands of antidepressants available, and individual GPs may have their own preferences and reasons for which drug they prescribe. It is also important to understand that antidepressants are not all the same; they work differently in the brain and so there may be cases where the first prescribed antidepressant may not be effective. If this is the case, the GP could switch to another type. In any event, antidepressants can take up to two weeks to produce any improvement and the full effect may not be seen for four to six weeks.

It is important that the patient sticks to taking the antidepressant at the recommended dosage and recommended times. However, if a carer is not present at the consultation, not all patients may be willing to share details with the carer concerning the taking of their medication. There is a danger that some patients may decide to stop taking them altogether because they feel better, or they may only take them when they feel the need rather than sticking to the recommended daily dose. There have been cases where patients have taken more than the prescribed dosage, wrongly believing it would have a quicker effect.

One of the main reasons for patients not continuing with medication is adverse side effects. Some patients may not be able to tolerate the side effects of the medication because it makes them feel worse, so they decide to stop taking them. If this is the case, it is important that the patient should go back to their GP and tell them what has happened. Patients' attitudes towards antidepressant treatment may be influenced by what they have seen or read in the media and on websites regarding the possible adverse side effects of taking antidepressants. Much also rests on the information the GP has given to the patient. How long might it take before the medication yields any improvement in symptoms? What are the benefits and possible adverse side effects? And what might happen if the patient decides to discontinue the medication? As one patient noted: 'I don't think there is enough explanation. I've seen three GPs and none of them actually explained what the tablets were that they were giving me. Just take them; they'll make you feel better after a few weeks.'[13]

It has been noted that patients have more confidence in their treatment when the GP provides more detailed information about the nature and effects of antidepressants. This was more likely to lead to patients sticking to taking the medication as instructed by the GP.[13]

Not knowing how or if the patient is taking the medication may be a cause of concern for the carer. You may have reason to suspect that the patient is not following the GP's instructions. But if there is an issue of confidentiality, how can the carer try to ensure that the patient is taking their medication in the right way?

The Royal College of Psychiatrists recognizes the role of the carer concerning medication by advising doctors that:

'Very often the carer will have a role in assisting with medication compliancy and this role should be discussed and agreed with the carer. In such cases the carer needs full details of the medications, dosages and frequency of application. A copy of the care plan should be given to the carer wherever possible . . .'

Despite this official advice, the issue of confidentiality may still prevent the GP from involving the carer as part of the treatment team. In these circumstances, you could make an appointment with the GP to express your concerns that the patient is not following their advice.

Part 6:

WHAT HAPPENS IF THE TREATMENT GIVEN BY THE GP IS NOT HELPING

If the first prescribed antidepressant has no significant effect, the GP has the option of switching to a different type, but even this does not guarantee recovery. As the weeks pass and there are no signs of a reduction in symptoms, the patient may begin to lose faith in their GP's ability to cure them. With the medication not being effective, the loss of the patient's hope of a rapid recovery may deepen the depression to the point where the deteriorating patient may be considered as treatment resistant. It is at this point that, ideally, a referral from a GP to a mental health team is good practice. This would signal to the patient that they will be seeing experts, with the hope and expectation that they will be able to come up with a treatment that works.

Mental health teams have a range of specialists, including psychiatrists, community psychiatric nurses, occupational therapists, talking therapists, social workers and support workers. The team will decide which of these people will be the best to help with each individual case of depression.

There may be cases where the team offer a 'carer's assessment' to see how carers are coping, and whether there is additional help that can be offered. The National Institute for Health and Care Excellence (NICE) advises that carers will receive: 'An assessment by social services of a carer's physical and mental health and their needs as a carer. Every person aged 16 years and older who cares for someone on a regular basis has the right to ask for a carer's assessment. There should be a written carer's plan, which is given to the carer' (NICE December 2011).

Under the care of the mental health team, patients may prefer either to try new medication or some form of talking therapy, or possibly both. The team would advise on what form of treatments they feel would be the most helpful for the patient.

If the team felt that the patient would also benefit from new medication, the psychiatrist would be responsible for arranging this. Through their specialized training, psychiatrists have more detailed knowledge of depression and its treatments than GPs; they have the skills to prescribe other medication, in addition to antidepressants, which may be more successful. However, this means another wait to see if these new drugs will work. If you are able to accompany the patient, you can play an important role at this critical stage by reporting the behavioural patterns of the patient, allowing the psychiatrist to have a more informed picture of the patient's condition and progress.

In cases where talking therapy has not helped, the medication is not working and there are signs that the patient may be seriously deteriorating, the mental health team may recommend that the patient be admitted to hospital for observation.

There may be cases where, as a last resort, the team suggest electroconvulsive therapy. This is a treatment that can work for some, and, if it does, it can bring the patient out of the illness in a relatively short space of time.

Electroconvulsive therapy is a safe treatment. Electrodes are placed on either side of the patient's head. The patient is then given a short-acting general anaesthetic and a small electric current is passed through the brain for a few seconds. There are a number of issues regarding this particular treatment and the psychiatrist should fully inform the patient – and, just as importantly, the carer – of what to expect in terms of benefit and risk.

The effectiveness of the carer with the treatment-resistant patient

Deep into the illness and with no recovery in sight, the patient may begin to experience a deeper sense of hopelessness and become increasingly demoralized by their condition. They may become the least responsive to loving help and sympathy. Your efforts to try and help the patient at this time are more likely to adversely affect you rather than improve the patient. Carers at this stage tend to become more stressed than at any time during the course of the patient's illness. Some may be at risk of becoming depressed themselves by this time. Although this period may be difficult, most carers decide it is better to keep their feelings to themselves, especially any suggestion of anger, so as to avoid worsening the patient's condition.[2] It is therefore important for you to have someone you can turn to for emotional support to help you through what is likely to be a challenging time.

Suicide

The longer time goes by without hope of recovery, the greater grows the risk that the patient may be seriously thinking about committing suicide. This is likely to become a major source of worry and concern for you.

Most people who suffer from depression will increasingly think about suicide at some point, and some may talk about their feelings but go no further than that. However, if the patient and carer can talk openly about these suicidal thoughts and feelings, it can save a life. Begin by reassuring them that their life is very important to you, the family and close friends.

The Depression Alliance website offers the following advice:

> Don't be afraid to ask them if they are suicidal, and try to reassure them that feeling or thinking the future is hope

less does not make it so in reality. If they have suicidal intentions, or have attempted suicide, call in other people (a GP, emergency services, social services) to help them and you with the situation. You can also contact The Samaritans.

However hard it may seem to look after a person who is suicidal, the fact that you are showing you care will have a positive impact.

There can be cases where the person with depression may be at such a risk of seriously harming themselves that the mental health team might decide that the only option is to use the powers of the Mental Health Act. After a very careful assessment, the person with depression can be admitted to hospital without their consent in order to keep them safe. This is commonly known as 'sectioning' people, since it is the application of a particular section of the act which allows people to be admitted against their will. There are a lot of safeguards in place to ensure that this power is not used in a way that is harmful to the patient.

Part 7:

RECOVERY AND RELAPSE PREVENTION

Preventing a relapse back into depression after recovery is a very important issue. An unwanted situation is the patient relapsing back into depression and again creating stress for the carer.

Relapse prevention strategies can help patients avoid relapse altogether or ensure they have fewer and shorter episodes of the illness. Carers can be very important in assisting with many relapse prevention strategies and spotting early warning signs that the patient may be heading for a relapse.

Recovery is generally defined as the disappearance of the major symptoms for at least two consecutive months. The three features most frequently judged by patients to be very important in determining recovery were the presence of positive mental health attitudes such as optimism and self-confidence; a return to one's 'normal self'; and a return to a usual level of functioning.[14] Some patients may show an improvement but still exhibit various symptoms. In any event, the period of time after recovery and how it is managed is just as crucial for carer and patient as the first episode of the illness.

There is a tendency for patients to believe that depression was an experience that has been overcome and will never be repeated. Some may be on a high, celebrating their recovery, and may become overconfident in their newfound energy, such that they start overdoing things, which can result in them becoming stressed and fatigued. You may need to encourage them not make any really important decisions – for example, if they are unhappy in a job or under pressure to make such decisions – until they have recovered enough to be able to do this. Carer and patient need to be aware that recovery is fragile and full recovery is an ongoing process.

As many as 80 per cent of recovered patients relapse between six to nine months after recovery and remain vulnerable to further relapses for several years. With this high possibility of relapse, you need to be vigilant in recognizing signs of symptoms returning.

One way of spotting early warning signs of possible relapse can be remembering the behaviour of the patient prior to the first episode of the illness and identifying any features that were present at that time.

Sliding into depression in the first place may have been caused simply by a steady increase in levels of anxiety and negative thinking over a period of time. But after recovery, it can take only the faintest of triggers – what would normally be considered as only a minor adverse event – to raise levels of anxiety and potentially lead in turn to another episode of depression.

You may need to help persuade the patient that it is important to receive effective ongoing treatment. Patients should continue on medication. However, there is no guarantee that medication alone will prevent a relapse; other forms of treatment need to be in place. The patient may still be under the mental health team at this stage. There is strong evidence suggesting that in addition to remaining on medication, talking therapy is helpful in order to prevent a relapse. CBT is the talking therapy most often used but it may not suit everyone. A number of alternative talking therapies are available. In any event, patients need good-quality talking therapies not only to get them better but also to teach them strategies as to how to stay that way. The mental health team will be able to inform you and the person you are caring for about which services are available, and their likely benefits.

Some patients may initially have negative feelings concerning talking therapy; they may feel it is too much of a struggle and lack the motivation to attend therapy sessions. Another issue is that the effectiveness of CBT or other talking therapies depends on the relationship that the patient and therapist are able to build with one another. Any therapy may not be effective if the therapist fails to tailor the treatment to the needs of the individual patient; patients may sense then that they and the therapist are not on the same wavelength. Should this happen, the patient will probably think, and with some justification, that attending further sessions would be pointless. However, it may be possible for the patient to switch therapists or the type of therapy until the right one is found.

If affordable, another option could be to see a specialist therapist on a private basis. In any event, for any talking therapy to be effective, the patient is likely to need a number of appointments. Talking therapy will help the patient to make the necessary changes in their lifestyle and their way of viewing what is important in their world in order to potentially reduce the risk and severity of relapse.

If a relapse does occur, perhaps the only source of comfort is that the duration of the relapse for some people is generally much shorter than the first episode. Should it happen, remind the patient that they will recover as they did before.

How levels of anxiety can affect the recovering patient

It has been previously explained that anxiety and depression are strongly linked and that high levels of anxiety make depression a physically uncomfortable experience for many. After recovery from the first episode, and for no apparent reason, symptoms of anxiety can strike without warning at any time, even when things seem to be going well. Because some people associate the uncomfortable physical feelings of anxiety with depression, they may believe that they are heading for another episode of the illness. If this belief goes unchallenged, there is a serious risk of a slide back into depression.[15] Therefore, if you are aware that the person is experiencing such feelings, you could explain to them that it is more likely to be only a level of anxiety rather than depression, and realizing this could help to change their attitude to their present situation and might help to prevent a slide into a full relapse.

Part 8:

CARING FOR THE CARER

It is well recognized that carers need help and support to enable them to get through the almost relentless period of caring by maintaining their own health and well-being both mentally and physically. There are times where perhaps you should consider taking a step back from your situation and discover ways in which you could get back some of the enjoyment of living a happier life without totally abandoning the patient.

As one carer began to realize:

'I have to take care of me. I'm important for myself and my family, too. '

couldn't live my own life because I was too preoccupied with theirs. I told them, and I said, "I cried a tub full of tears and it never changed a thing." I still care. I care about them, but I cannot live like this, I mean live my life for them completely. That's too much you know."[16]

You need to understand that you can only do so much and accept what can and can't be controlled. In order to avoid a physical and mental collapse, it is important to pace yourself by not trying to do too much, because you may be caring for a lengthy period of time. Even if time is limited, doing something just for yourself will be helpful.

But if you are starting to experience problems with your own health due to high levels of stress, then this is the time for action. Visiting the GP is the first step. The GP may offer some form of treatment, which can include referring you on to other healthcare professionals,

such as counsellors or other talking therapists. Carers may appreciate an opportunity
to speak to a therapist who they can trust and
where they can be more open about what
they are going through. Other people that
carers may feel able to confide in and discuss
their problems with would be sympathetic
and understanding friends or relatives.
Contacting the local carers' advice centre can
also be helpful when things are becoming
too much to handle. These centres provide
helpful information on how carers can look
after themselves: how the carer can attain
a level of freedom, have a life of their own
and find time for themselves. Depending on
circumstances, these advice centres can also
organize ways for the carer to take a respite
break away from their caring role.

There is growing recognition by the UK gov-
ernment of the contribution of carers. The
Department of Health Carers' Strategy 2008
includes a future commitment that: 'Carers
will be respected as expert carer partners
and will have access to the integrated and

personalised services they need to support them in their caring role', and that 'carers will be supported to stay mentally and physically well and treated with dignity'.

The Carers' Strategy also includes the commitment that young carers need to have: 'The support they need to learn, develop and thrive to enjoy positive childhoods.' Recognizing the need for 'Improvements for young carers specifically', it continues, 'it must ensure their opportunity to enjoy their childhoods and to learn, develop and thrive as other children do is properly protected.'

Part 9:

THE POSITIVES OF CARING

'I feel the capacity to care is the thing which gives life its deepest significance.'

Pablo Casals

That you will be unable to lift the patient's depression completely may be the reality, but that does not mean you cannot make a positive difference that can benefit the patient. Good quality of care can help the recovery process; it can lead the patient to believe they are cared for, loved and valued. It has also been found that in cases where carers are coping well in their role, the patient's depressive episode may last for a shorter time.[17]

Another important and positive example of the carer's value is that with the risk of suicide in depression, carers can be life-savers. In comparison, patients who live alone have higher rates of attempted and completed suicide.

Research suggests carers who have a good sense of their own value and worth tend to interpret life events as positive challenges and also have the ability to find positive meaning to their role. Although there will always be some difficult times, carers can learn from their experience by gaining an awareness of their inner strengths, becoming more self-confident, growing as a person, learning new things about themselves.[4]

Carers who can develop a positive appraisal and acceptance of the situation are more likely to suffer less stress and maintain a greater sense of competence, satisfaction and self-esteem.

It must also be remembered that depressed

patients do eventually recover, and this is another factor that can help keep you going through the really difficult times.

KEY POINTS TO REMEMBER

♦ Know the nature of depression and how it affects the patient

♦ Encourage the depressed person to talk about what they are going through as early as possible

♦ Don't be alone – find all the help you can from understanding and sympathetic family and friends

♦ Find advice and support from local carers' organizations

♦ Encourage the patient to seek treatment

KEY POINTS TO REMEMBER

◆ Become involved as part of the treatment team with the help of the GP and other healthcare professionals

◆ Make time for yourself and look after your own health

◆ Accept that there is only so much you can do to help the patient to recover

◆ Recovery is an ongoing process – be prepared for setbacks

◆ Try to encourage the patient to seek ongoing treatment after recovery

USEFUL WEBSITES FOR ADVICE AND SUPPORT

If you do not have access to a computer, your local library can help.

Carers' advice
www.carersuk.org
www.carers.org
www.mind.org.uk
www.rethink.org
www.nhs.uk/carersdirect
www.depressionalliance.org

For carers living in Scotland
www.actionondepression.org

USEFUL WEBSITES FOR ADVICE AND SUPPORT

For carers living in Wales
www.journeysonline.org.uk

For carers living in Northern Ireland
www.aware-ni.org.uk

Young carers
www.youngcarers.net
www.youngcarersmatter.org
www.carers.org
www.barnados.org.uk – the Barnardo's
Willow Project that supports young carers

Suicide prevention
www.helpguide.org
www.samaritans.org

Finding a qualified psychotherapist or counsellor
www.psychotherapy.org.uk
www.bacp.co.uk

REFERENCES

1. Ryff, C. D. and B. Singer, 'Psychological Well-being: Meaning, Measurement, and Implications for Psychotherapy Research', *Psychotherapy and Psychosomatics* 65(1) (January–February 1996): 14–23.

2. Highet, N., B. G. McNair, T. A. Davenport and I. B. Hickie, '"How Much More Can We Lose?" Carer and Family Perspectives on Living with a Person with Depression', *Medical Journal of Australia* 181(7) (2004): 6.

3. Harris, T. J., N. Pistrang and C. Barker, 'Couples' Experiences of the Support Process in Depression: A Phenomenological Analysis', *Psychology and Psychotherapy: Theory, Research and Practice* 79 (2006): 1–21.

REFERENCES

4. Veltman, A., J. I. Cameron and D. E. Stewart, 'The Experience of Providing Care to Relatives with Chronic Mental Illness', *The Journal of Nervous and Mental Disease* 190 (2002): 108–14.

5. Grant, G. and M. Nolan, 'Informal Carers: Sources and Concomitants of Satisfaction', *Health and Social Care in the Community* 1(3) (May 1993): 147–59.

6. Karp, D. A. *Speaking of Sadness* (New York and Oxford: Oxford University Press, 1996).

7. Karp, D. and V. Tanarugsachock, 'Mental Illness, Caregiving, and Emotion Management', *Qualitative Health Research* 10(1) (January 2000): 6–25.

8. Barney, L. J., K. M. Griffiths, H. Christensen and A.F. Jorm, 'Exploring the Nature of Stigmatising Beliefs about Depression and Health Seeking: Implications for Reducing Stigma', *BMC Public Health* 9 (2009): 61.

9. Holbourne, D. 'Helping a Husband or Wife over Depression', www.broadcaster.org.uk, accessed 9 October 2012.

10. Kadam, U. T., P. Croft, J. Mcleod and M. Hutchinson, 'A Qualitative Study of Patients'

Views on Anxiety and Depression', *British Journal of General Practice* 51 (2001): 375–80.

11. Department of Health, *Developing Services for Carers and Families of People with Mental Illness*, November 2002.

12. Tylee, A., 'Major Depressive Disorder (MDD) from the Patient's Perspective: Overcoming Barriers to Appropriate Care', *International Journal of Psychiatry in Clinical Practice* 5(1) (2001): 37–42.

13. Haslam, C., S. Brown, S. Atkinson and R. Haslam, 'Patients' Experiences of Medication for Anxiety and Depression: Effects on Working Life', *Family Practice* 21(2) (2004): 204–12.

14. Zimmerman, M., J. B. McGlinchey, M. A. Posternak, M. Friedman, N. Attiullah and D. Boerescu, 'How Should Remission from Depression be Defined? The Depressed Patient's Perspective', *American Journal of Psychiatry* 163 (2006): 148–50.

15. Cassin, S. E. and N. A. Rector, 'The Scarring Effects of Past Depression on Anxiety Sensitivity: Examining Risk for Depressive Relapse and Recurrence', *International*

REFERENCES

Journal of Cognitive Therapy 5(1) (2012): 18–27.

16. Badger, T. A., 'Family Members' Experiences Living with Members with Depression', *Western Journal of Nursing Research* 18(2) (April 1996): 149–71.

17. Keitner, G. I., I. W. Miller, N. B. Epstein, D. S. Bishop and A. E. Fruzetti, 'Family Functioning and the Course of Major Depression', *Comprehensive Psychiatry* 28(1) (January / February 1987): 54–64.